Manatee

Manatee

ON LOCATION

KATHY DARLING

PHOTOGRAPHS BY TARA DARLING

LOTHROP, LEE & SHEPARD BOOKS   NEW YORK

Text copyright © 1991 by Kathy Darling
Photographs copyright © 1991 by Tara Darling
All rights reserved. No part of this book may be reproduced or utilized in any form or by any means, electronic or mechanical, including photocopying, recording or by any information storage and retrieval system, without permission in writing from the Publisher. Inquiries should be addressed to Lothrop, Lee & Shepard Books, a division of William Morrow & Company, Inc., 105 Madison Avenue, New York, New York 10016. Printed in Singapore.

First Edition   1 2 3 4 5 6 7 8 9 10

Library of Congress Cataloging in Publication Data
Darling, Kathy. Manatee / Kathy Darling ; photographs by Tara Darling.
p.   cm. — (On location) Includes bibliographical references. Summary: Text and photographs describe the life history, physical characteristics, behavior, and underwater activities of the Florida manatee and how scientists and others are trying to save this endangered sea mammal.   ISBN 0-688-09030-3 — ISBN 0-688-09031-1 (lib. bdg.)   1. Manatees—Juvenile literature.   [1. Manatees.   2. Rare animals.] I. Darling, Tara, ill.   II. Title.   III. Series: Darling, Kathy. On location.   QL737.S63D37   1991
599.5'5—dc20   89-45904   CIP   AC

Dedicated to Sweetgums and Nick,
our adopted manatees:
Long may they live in peace.

ACKNOWLEDGMENTS

Dr. Jesse White, D.V.M., marine mammal veterinarian; adjunct professor, University of Florida; founder of the Florida Manatee Research and Educational Foundation. Dr. White was responsible for the first successful captive breeding program for manatees and for the majority of our knowledge of the manatee's reproductive biological information. He provided the anatomical diagrams used on pages 18–19, based on drawings by Candace Hollinger taken from plates by J. Murie. Thank you, Dr. White, for your invaluable assistance and for checking the manuscript for accuracy.

Save the Manatee Club, especially Director Judith Vallee.

Nikon, Inc., for the generous loan of underwater cameras and lenses. All the photographs in this book were shot using Nikon equipment.

U.S. Fish and Wildlife Service and Florida Department of Natural Resources, Glen Curowan, U.S. Manatee Coordinator; Patrick Hagen, manager of the Crystal River Wildlife Refuge; Lori Price, Florida Bureau of Marine Research; and especially the rangers and volunteers whose devoted work in the field is helping to save manatees.

Florida Power and Light Company for providing us with much information and the aerial photograph on page 38.

The People of Crystal River, down-home friendly folks who LOVE manatees. Special thanks to Dick Myers of the Plantation Inn and Sam Lyons of the Plantation Inn Marina.

Homosassa Nature World for allowing us to photograph the manatees they are rehabilitating. And to aquarist Betsy Dearth for her special assistance.

Contents

A mother and her 6-month-old baby stay close togther.

Water 1 Baby

Crystal River, Florida
November 30
5 A.M.

At the head of the river was a mighty spring, pumping out 650 million gallons of clear, warm water every day. In the center of the spring, called the main boil, a three-thousand-pound cow manatee swam in circles. Below her lay more of the gigantic gray mammals, sleeping quietly in the bubbling warmth of the hot spring.

The cow had been circling all night, making high-pitched noises and thrashing her tail. In true manatee fashion, the others ignored her.

The cow was not ill; she was pregnant and in labor. Her restless circling stopped only when she rose to the surface to breathe air. Poking just her nostrils above water, the cow took two quick breaths. Then she began her slow circling again.

Now it was time for the baby to be born. The cow bent her sausage-shaped body forward, and a gray bubblelike object began to emerge from the birth canal on her lower abdomen. The manatee spun around and around till the birth sac broke. The head of a baby manatee was visible near her tail. Then, with one violent squeeze, the cow expelled the calf headfirst into the water.

A manatee baby is born knowing that it must breathe air and not water. It also knows where the air is and how to get there by itself.

The slate-gray calf, who would remain darker in color than his gray mother for about a month, was three feet long. Big for a new-born manatee, he weighed nearly eighty pounds.

From the moment of birth, the manatee calf was a good swimmer. He used his tail and his paddle-shaped flippers to move through the water, staying close to the surface and rising to breathe every twenty seconds. He was learning the rhythm of manatee breathing. With practice he would be able to hold his breath longer, surfacing every four minutes like his mother.

Unlike most land mammals, the newborn calf could see; and he could hear. And he could make noise!

He called to his mother, but she paid little attention. All through the morning she continued to circle in the spring, trying to expel the afterbirth and finish the birth process.

Later she would be a good mother. She would keep the baby close to her side for two years as they journeyed between the river and the sea with the changing seasons. The water baby would grow big on the sea cow's milk,

Mother manatees will nurse any hungry baby. Nipples are behind her flippers.

richer than that of a land cow. Mother and baby would "talk" almost constantly as the cow taught her calf how to survive. The two would take time for tag, keep away, and other games manatees play.

For forty-five million years there have been manatees in the shallow coastal waters of America. Perhaps there were once many thousands. Now there are only about 1,200 manatees left in Florida. And there are fewer each year. Could this little water baby be the last generation of his species? It is possible.

Officially on the endangered species list since 1973, the manatee has been difficult to protect. These nomads roam in muddy, shallow water from one sea-grass meadow to another in a unpredictable pattern. It is only with great difficulty that scientists have been able to discover some of the secrets of their underwater life.

Much of what we know about wild manatees comes from pioneer studies done by Dr. Daniel Hartman in the Crystal River of Florida. This unique place is perfect for manatee research. Warm springs and abundant food lure large numbers of manatees there in winter. The clear water makes it easy to study them.

Crystal River is now a national wildlife refuge, and in this protected spot manatees allow humans to get close. For two years my daughter, Tara, and I studied and photographed the manatees of Crystal River for this book, which is the first picture record of the gentle Florida manatee.

The first time I got into the water with wild manatees, I was scared. They are very big. Some of the biggest weigh twenty times more than I do. When I looked around, there were manatees everywhere. One of the gray monsters began to swim toward me! When he got close, he rolled over for a scratch. I laughed.

It doesn't take long to learn that manatees mean people no harm. Federal law forbids chasing or even touching manatees. But some of the manatees touched *us*. They seem to like people and it is impossible not to like them back.

Scientists have only recently begun to study manatees. Field observations have changed old views that were based on guesses. It was thought that a manatee baby needed help to take its first breath. In 1982, Dr. Jesse White, a veterinarian at the Miami Seaquarium, was the first to see a manatee being born. The calf

This baby manatee is enjoying a back scratch. The warty skin, which is found only in Crystal River youngsters, will disappear as the animal grows. It is caused by a virus like the one that causes chicken pox in humans.

emerged tail first and then swam unaided to the surface. A few years later, Dr. White saw another birth. He was surprised because this time the baby was born headfirst.

Much about the life history of the manatee is *still* not known. There are blanks to be filled in and mysteries to be solved. A lot, young scientists, waits for you.

13

Manatees munch weeds 8 hours a day. It takes 200 pounds of grass to fill a hungry sea cow.

What is a Manatee?

Manatees are marine mammals with a body form somewhere between those of a seal and a whale. They have no hind limbs, and their forelimbs have evolved into flippers. The manatee and its relative, the dugong, are called sirenians. They are the only marine mammals that eat plants. The Florida manatee is the largest vegetarian creature in the sea and is bigger than any land animal in America.

Although they live in the sea, manatees are not fish. Like humans, sea cows are mammals.

Scientists believe life on earth began in the sea about three billion years ago. After two and a half billion years some animals left the water to live on land. Then, forty-five million years ago, for reasons no one completely understands, some of these early mammals returned to life in the sea. Whales, seals, and manatees are descended from these land animals.

The manatees are not closely related to the carnivorous whales and seals they look so much like. They evolved from the same grass-eating land animal as the elephant.

Manatees still eat grass. The difference is that now they do it underwater. This all-grass diet limits where they can live. Manatees do not eat seaweed, kelp, or other deep-water plants because these are not grass but a form of algae. All grasses require sunlight, which can reach only about 15 feet below the surface. So manatees never leave the shallow waters close to shore.

Fossil evidence shows that once there were more than a dozen species of sea cows. In man's time there have been five. Steller's sea cow was exterminated in 1786. The remaining four—the Amazon, West African, and West Indian manatees and the dugong—have been hunted almost to extinction for meat, oil, skin, teeth, and even for "tears."

Manatees do not defend themselves. Even if they wanted to, they could not protect themselves very well. Since the sirenians evolved without any natural enemies, they never developed aggressive or defensive weapons. Manatees don't fight among themselves over food or breeding rights or territory. Nor are there any leaders. A manatee simply does not fight, even to save its baby or its own life!

The Florida manatee is one of the few aquatic animals that move freely between salt and fresh water. There are manatees on Florida's east and west coasts, but the two groups do not meet. In the spring, summer, and fall, manatees live alone, spending most of their time eating. In winter they gather in temporary herds at warm spring refuges. The only lasting bond that manatees form is that between cow and calf. Even that lasts only till the calf is weaned.

A subspecies of the West Indian manatee, the Florida manatee is slightly larger than others in the species. Their scientific name is *Trichechus manatus latirostris*. The first part is Latin for "hairy," *manatus* means "breast" in a language of the Caribbean Indians, and *latirostris* means "broad faced" in Latin.

Manatee *3* Anatomy

Manatee bones are not like the bones of other mammals. They are unusually heavy and solid all the way through. Most mammals' bones are hollow, and red blood cells are produced in the center. A manatee's red blood cells are produced in its spinal column. Dense bones make a manatee sink, an advantage for bottom feeding.

The spine contains from 47 to 54 bones. It extends into the enormous muscular tail, which provides the power for swimming. The flippers are not used for swimming and are held against the body during speed bursts. Flippers help steer or are used to walk on the bottom. You can see the bones for five separate "fingers" in the skeleton, which looks like that of a human arm. The fingernails are the only outward evidence that the flipper was once something quite different.

There are no leg bones at all. Where land mammals have a pelvis, the manatee has a tiny L-shaped bone embedded in the muscle.

A strange thing about the manatee's spinal column is that it contains only six neck vertebrae. All other mammals, even whales, have seven. These disklike bones are so closely joined that a manatee cannot turn its head.

Manatees continue to grow throughout their lives. There is no such thing as a full-grown manatee. As the animal gets bigger, new bone is added to support the weight.

Males and females are about the same size,

SKELETAL DIAGRAM

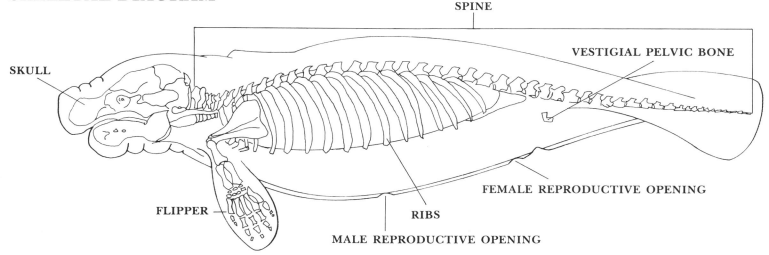

which is unusual in large mammals. It is not easy to tell the sexes apart. The reproductive organs are internal, and the nipples of the female are hidden under the flipper. The only visible difference between the sexes is the location of the reproductive openings.

Females are sexually mature at seven to nine years and can bear young for the rest of their lives. They have no fixed breeding season and will mate with numerous males. One or sometimes two young are born after a thirteen-month pregnancy. Calves nurse for two years from thumb-sized nipples. Males mature sexually at six or seven years, mate with many females, and do not assist in raising young.

In manatees, the digestive and respiratory systems are not connected. Babies can nurse underwater, and adults can swallow food without getting water into their breathing passages.

The muscular lungs are protected by rock-like ribs and run almost the entire length of the back. Surprisingly, the lungs are no bigger than a human's lungs in proportion to body size. The muscle called the diaphragm, which pushes against the lungs to expel air, does not press upward as in most animals. Located between the manatee's lungs, the diaphragm

RESPIRATORY AND DIGESTIVE DIAGRAM

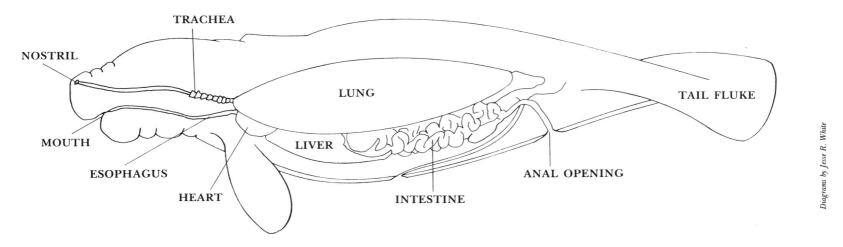

TRACHEA

NOSTRIL

LUNG

TAIL FLUKE

MOUTH

LIVER

ESOPHAGUS

HEART

INTESTINE

ANAL OPENING

Diagrams by Jesse R. White

presses them outward against the ribs.

The muscles of the lungs are used to control flotation. A lungful of air can be squeezed into a small area. The body displaces less water and it sinks. When the manatee wants to rise, it releases the pressure on the air, the lungs fill again, and the animal floats.

A digestive gland in the manatee's stomach coats chewed food with mucus to prevent irritation. Additional mucus glands are located in the large intestine, which can be up to 150 feet long. Most digestion takes place there, using bacteria to break down the cellulose in grass. This "hind gut" digestion,

also found in elephants and horses, results in the production of enormous quantities of gas!

Manatee skin is very wrinkled and up to two inches thick. It is so tough, arrows will not pierce it. Amazon Indians used manatee leather for their war shields. The skin is constantly sloughing off in large sheets. This makes the manatees look diseased, but the shedding is normal and prevents the buildup of algae and parasites. Lice, barnacles, and remoras, the same kind of sucker fish that attach to sharks, are all commonly found on manatees.

19

Six Senses

Humans have five senses: vision, hearing, touch, taste, and smell. The manatee has a sixth: smell-taste.

VISION: Manatee vision is a technicolor show. What a manatee can see in the water is probably very similar to what you can see wearing a diving mask. After millions of years in the sea, manatees' eyes, once designed for land vision, have changed so that they can focus clearly underwater and are not irritated by salt. Glands close to the eye produce an oil, and a membrane spreads the oil across the eye to protect it from salt. When some kinds of sea cows are taken out of the water, the protective oil hardens into little balls. Australian aborigines thought these were "tears" with magical powers. Dugongs are still killed for their magic tears.

Eyelashes, which keep out dirt and dust on land, are absent. So are eyelids. But a manatee can still close its tiny blue eyes by tightening a ring of muscles called a sphincter, which closes up like the lens of a camera. This is handy because, like us, manatees sleep with their eyes closed.

Manatees can easily spot objects (like delicious weeds) at a distance. But the clumsy cows lack accurate depth perception at close range and turn into one-ton klutzes, often accidentally poking themselves or bumping into one another.

They have not lost the ability to see out of

Instead of an eyelid, the manatee uses a ring of strong muscles to shut its eye.

water. Occasionally manatees nibble on shoreline grasses and overhanging trees. In Florida, sea cows do not get totally out of the water to eat, but we discovered they do in less populated parts of Central America.

HEARING: Behind the eye is a hole about as big around as the end of a sharpened pencil ($\frac{1}{40}$th of an inch). This tiny opening is the manatee's ear. Like most marine animals, manatees don't have external ears. Ears like ours operate very poorly in water even though sounds travel farther in water than in air and four times as fast. Hearing well underwater requires a different type of "sound receiver." Marine mammals receive sounds through the entire skull, not only the ears, and can accurately locate underwater noises.

Manatees are very sensitive to sounds. The click of a camera lens ten feet away, or the sound of Scuba divers breathing, can disturb them.

When they are submerged, sirenians are able to detect sounds made above the water. At night, before they surface to breathe, they rely on their sensitive hearing to warn them of approaching motorboats. Small planes flying over the Crystal River Wildlife Refuge sometimes wake a sleeping herd and cause them to swim off in a panic. At Homosassa's Nature World the keeper calls manatees with a little clicker. They have learned that the clicker noise means snacks and immediately rush to her side for a handout of horse chow or lettuce.

Manatees also create and transmit sounds. Humans can hear their high-pitched calls several hundred feet away. Nobody knows over what distance they can communicate with each other in manatee language. How these sounds are produced is a mystery. Manatees have no vocal cords. There is no movement of mouth, lips, or throat. Nor is any air or water taken in or pushed out.

Each manatee's voice is unique. A mother can identify her calf by the sound of its voice and will respond only to her own baby's cry. And every sound has a definite meaning. A frightened manatee emits a piercing high-pitched scream. Courting males make soft piggy grunts to attract the attention of fe-

*The presence of divers doesn't always alarm manatees. They seem
to enjoy a friendly patting or scratching.*

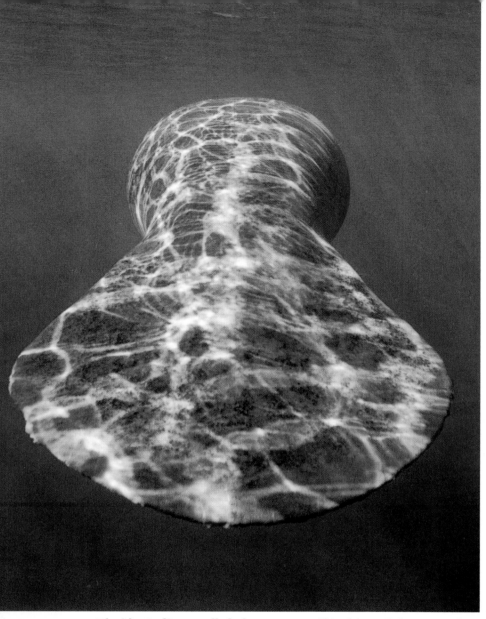

Florida Indians called the manatee "big beaver" because of its wide, flat tail.

males. But except for communication between cow and calf, which is frequent, manatees are generally quiet animals.

TOUCH: A great deal of a manatee's life is solitary. Groups or herds are formed only in winter at the warm-water refuges. Then, as if to make up for lost time, the manatees have constant body contact. Even manatee games, although always friendly, are usually contact sports with plenty of bumping and shoving.

Manatees like to touch and be touched. They rub against objects. They nuzzle one another. In places like Crystal River, where they have come to trust humans, some beg divers for a pat. Cows and calves are always in contact, through either talk or touch. A sleeping baby rests on its mother's tail or back. When swimming with its mother the baby places its muzzle on her body.

The thick, wrinkly skin is very sensitive. And it is covered with large stiff hairs. The hair surprised scientists so much that they gave manatees the name *Trichechus*, which means "to have hair." The big hairs, spaced about an inch apart, don't give warmth but detect changes in currents even if the water is moving only three inches an hour. The hairs can also reveal the direction of a moving object and its speed and size.

For safety, manatees in a herd tend to breathe in unison. The hairs pick up vibrations and pressure waves when one manatee moves, alerting the others to rise and breathe.

The vibrissae, or whiskers, are specialized hairs of extreme sensitivity. Those farthest from the mouth are flexible, like a cat's whiskers, and those close to the lips are sharp and stiff, like a porcupine's quills. A manatee uses the bristles on its upper lip to find and identify food and to explore the bottom by nuzzling items in its path. So sensitive are the vibrissae that the manatee can locate food in muddy water or in the dark of night.

TASTE: Manatees taste the same flavors that humans do—sweet, bitter, sour, and salt—but with hundreds of times greater sensitivity. Manatees have well-developed taste buds and equally strong food preferences. Near the Crystal River there is a patch of water lilies. The manatees eat all the plants around this patch and never touch the lilies, although they are edible.

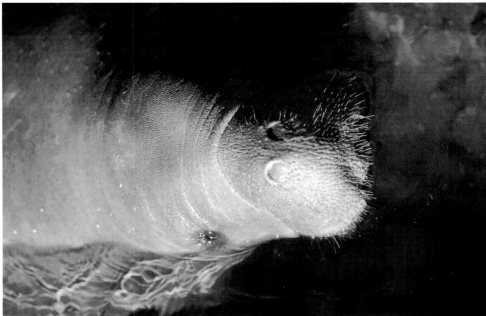

Manatee nostrils are like little trap doors, opened only for breathing. Top: nostrils opened. Bottom: nostrils shut.

25

The canals of southern Florida are choked with water hyacinths. It was hoped that manatees would help control them. Unfortunately, manatees don't like water hyacinths any more than water lilies.

SMELL: Underwater, manatees keep their nostrils clamped tightly shut and cannot smell as land animals do. Above water, manatees probably can distinguish odors. They are sometimes seen eating plants hanging over the water.

SMELL-TASTE: "Smell-taste" is the manatee's sixth sense. It is not a combination of smell and taste as we know them. We associate smell with airborne substances and taste with solid or liquid substances placed in the mouth. Just beyond the limits of our power of detection lies a different sense, one based on waterborne odors. This odor map guides many animals, and it is a map with a huge advantage over sight. It can be used at night or in the dark of the ocean depths.

One sign that manatees possess such a sense is their scent glands. Sirenians leave scent "messages" by rubbing those glands over a rock or sunken log. To read the messages, a manatee moves its muzzle across this "message center." Scientists call this behavior smell-tasting. Manatees identify one another by nuzzling the back and smell-tasting. If a female ready to breed has been at the message center, a bull can track her through the water by following her chemical trail.

Smell-taste is also a navigational aid. By analyzing the smell-taste—the amount of salt and other chemicals in the water, the temperature, the current—and perhaps magnetic and electronic signals, a manatee can find "home."

26

This manatee is having a smell-taste at a message center.

Marching Teeth 5

Did you ever dream of teeth that would never need filling, drilling, or pulling? Ones that would replace themselves when they wore out?

Manatees have just such teeth. Some lower vertebrates, such as snakes, can replace a fang if it breaks off. Sharks are regular tooth factories. One species can make a whole new set in less than a week. But of all the mammals, only the manatee has an endless supply of teeth.

All through a manatee's life new teeth form at the back of the jaw and migrate forward, conveyor-belt fashion. The big grinding molars, the only kind of teeth an adult manatee has, wear down as they move toward the front of the mouth, where they eventually fall out. They can do this because the manatee's unique teeth have no roots anchored in the jawbones. Instead, the huge molars, which are shaped like crinkle-cut french fries, are connected to one another and to the back of the jaws by strong ligaments.

Baby manatees are born with a full set of teeth. A calf has even more teeth than an adult—premolars as well as molars. As long as the calf nurses, the teeth do not move. Only when it starts to eat plants do the teeth begin to march. Apparently it is chewing that starts the process.

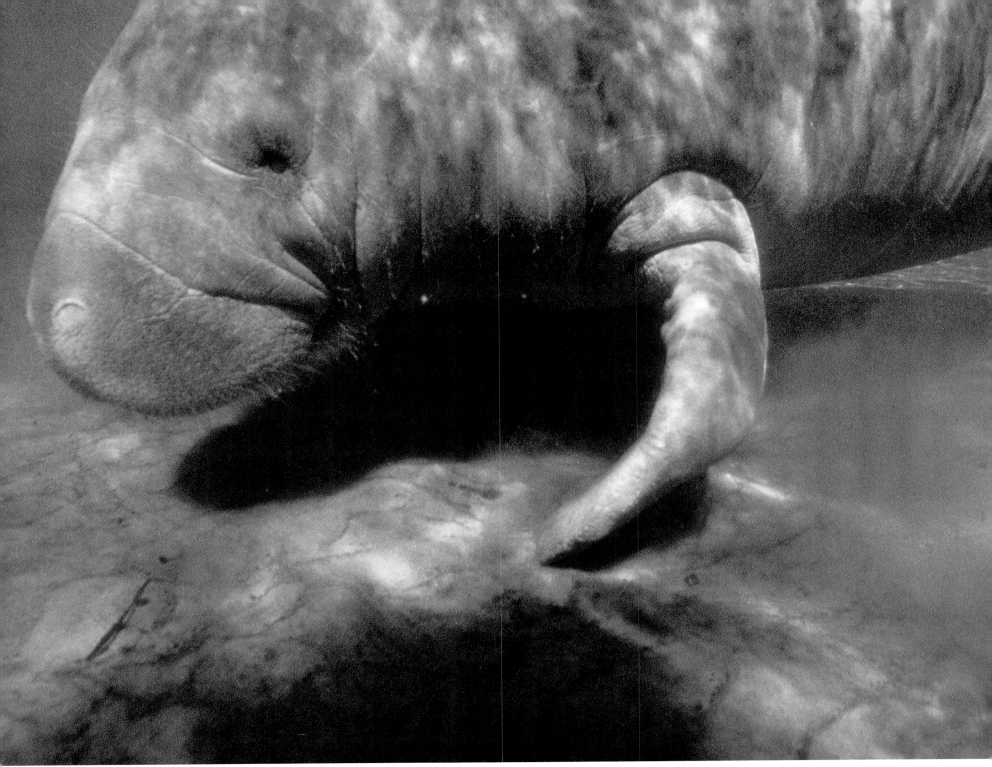

Flippers are handy tools when digging for tasty roots.

The manatee's marching teeth were discovered by accident in 1975. A researcher studying Amazonian manatees in Brazil was cleaning the pools where they were kept and she found a tooth. Over the next four years she found sixty-six more teeth the seven manatees had shed. From these teeth she determined that the marching teeth move about 1 or 2 millimeters (.04 to .08 inches) a month.

Why animals that eat only soft, wet grasses needed an endless supply of teeth was quite a mystery. One sirenian, the dugong, did not have marching teeth, which was even more puzzling. Scientists began to look for clues. Dugongs live only in the sea. West Indian and West African manatees alternate between salt and fresh water; the Amazonian manatee stays in fresh water all its life. They had three habitats, and each habitat provided a different diet. Since teeth are directly related to food, this looked like the key to the riddle. And it was.

Dugongs eat sea grasses, whereas manatees eat mostly freshwater grasses. Freshwater grasses contain spicules, or tiny particles of abrasive silica, which wear out teeth. The silica is a form of defense that makes the plants less appetizing, less digestible, and less nutritious to plant eaters.

In the sea the only large plant eaters are the sirenians and giant marine turtles, but many animals compete for freshwater grasses. The plants that have survived are those that developed defenses.

Over centuries manatees evolved ways to get around those defenses. Replaceable teeth help cope with abrasive silica. So do glands that coat swallowed food with mucus to protect the lining of the digestive system.

Poison is another plant defense. The manatee has in turn evolved its own poison-control center. In the intestine are microbes that help to detoxify the plants' chemical weapons. A lot more study is needed before we understand exactly how sea cows change poisonous grasses into safe food.

Manatees are called herbivores, or vegetarians, but sometimes they eat meat. Millions of bacteria used to break down cellulose are digested along with the plants. In the wild, manatees swallow little crabs, snails, and other animals that cling to the grasses they eat. This may not be accidental; fishermen in Jamaica have reported seeing manatees eating fish caught in nets. Captive manatees are known to like raw fish. Sometimes keepers trick them into taking pills by wrapping them in a fish treat.

This animal protein may be a necessary supplement to a grass diet that is low in food value. In order to get enough nourishment, a manatee must eat two hundred pounds of grass every day. More than half of the carbohydrates in grass are found in the roots or rhizomes. Manatees dig through the mud with flippers and snouts for these favorite foods.

Flippers are used for digging but seldom in eating. A manatee uses a unique method of getting its food into its mouth. The manatee finds a clump of grass; then its flexible snout, which is strengthened with horny pads, extends forward. The lips wrap around the plant, securing it with the vibrissae. Then with a rippling movement, the plant is ripped away and passed along the snout, into the mouth and the grinding molars.

After eating, a manatee always cleans its teeth. Trapped weeds and bits of dirt can be

The flexible snout is studded with hairlike vibrissae that grasp and guide food to the horny pads of the mouth, which are visible in these unusual photos.

so irritating that some animals go into frenzies. Each manatee has a special tooth-cleaning technique. We watched one pick up rocks, roll them around in its mouth, and spit them out. A small female opened her mouth in a sort of yawn and rocked back and forth to wash out irritants. The littlest baby we studied put his flipper in his mouth to sweep away trapped particles. The lazy ones just used little fish as living toothbrushes.

Underwater Blimps

Manatees not only look fat, they are fat. About 20 percent of the animal's weight is fat. Manatees wear a jacket of fat and have additional blubber packed around the heart, nestled against the stomach, and deposited among the muscles. You'd think that with all that fat, manatees would float like corks, but they don't. Their heavy bones counteract the buoyancy of the blubber.

Fat is healthy for a manatee. Skinny fish can live in cold water. But a skinny manatee couldn't survive. That's because a manatee is a mammal, and unlike fish, mammals need to keep a constant body temperature. The manatee's 97.5° temperature is very close to our own 98.6°F (37°C).

Water conducts heat away from the body about twenty times more quickly than air, so all aquatic mammals have trouble keeping warm. Although manatees and dugongs live where water temperatures are 70° to 75°F (21° to 23.8°C), maintaining body heat is still a problem. Fat helps. It acts as insulation, keeping the heat in.

The size of the manatee is another heat-saving adaptation. A big animal loses heat more slowly than a small one. A small body, even if it were very fat, wouldn't conserve heat as efficiently. Nature favors "underwater blimps" like whales, walrus, seals, and manatees.

The gentle, slow-moving "blimp" that looks

Manatee bodies are surprisingly flexible.

clumsy in photographs is really graceful and powerful. With water supporting its enormous weight, the manatee can turn somersaults, do head and tail stands and barrel rolls, and even swim upside down.

Fat is more than an insulator, it is an emergency food supply. When grass is plentiful, manatees eat as much as they can, storing the extra as fat. In autumn, manatees spend more time eating. They put on hundreds of pounds of fat to get them through the cold season.

In winter, plants don't grow as fast and food becomes scarce. But manatees can survive on their fat. By spring, when they head out to sea again, manatees have used up their fat reserves. But they are alive and healthy.

Because of their remarkable fat-storage system, manatees can fast (go without eating anything) for long periods. Some Florida manatees have been observed fasting for a month. Amazon manatees fast for six months every year. In the dry season, the Amazon River gets too shallow for safety, and the manatees must migrate to lakes where there is deep water. In those lakes there is safety from hunters, but no grass to eat. During the long fast, conserving energy is important.

Manatees are good at conserving energy. They have a slow metabolism—one of the lowest among mammals. The metabolism rate describes the body's efficiency in using energy. If cars were animals, you could say a Porsche has a high metabolism because it uses lots of gas and a Volkswagen has a slow metabolism because it gets better gas mileage. The metabolism of a manatee is four times more efficient than that of a human.

Manatees *need* to be fuel efficient. The plants they eat are low in calories (food energy). If the water temperature drops below 68°F (20°C) manatees use up most of the calories just keeping warm.

In cold weather the energy required to find food and digest it would be greater than the calories in the food. So manatees may not eat when the water or even the air is too cold. Cold air breathed into the lungs lowers the body temperature.

In extreme cold, manatees sometimes die. Scientists think that they stop eating, living instead on stored fat. If they use up their insulating fat, manatees might go into shock or catch pneumonia. Either one could be fatal.

During cold times, manatees try to control

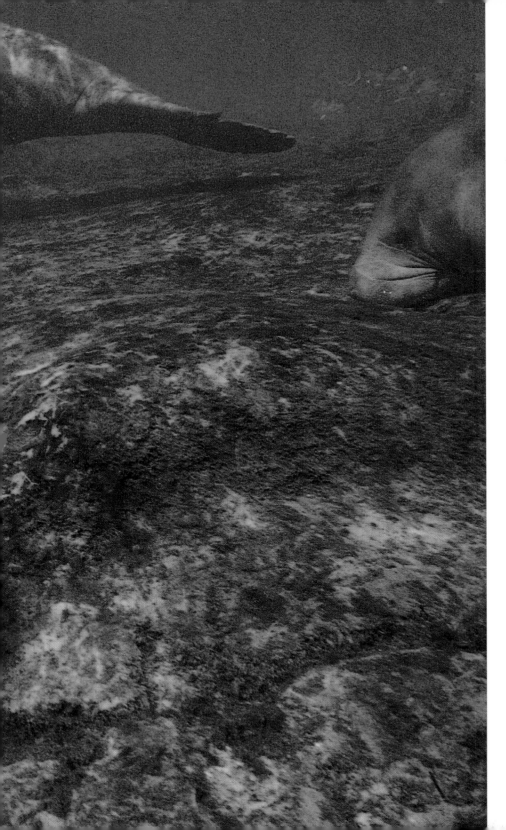

heat loss by feeding when the water is warmest. In Crystal River the sea cows sleep in the warmest part of the spring on cold nights. In midafternoon, when the sun has warmed the river water, they move out to feed. When the sun sets, the river water begins to cool again and the sea cows return to the hot spring where the water is always a constant 72°F (22°C). In warmer weather manatees do not keep a set schedule like this. They are endogenous, a word used by biologists to describe animals that don't keep regular hours. Predicting what a manatee will do at a specific hour is difficult.

One thing manatees are predictable about is gathering in warm water when the weather is cold. Some leave the cold sea for naturally warm places. In areas without hot springs, they take advantage of high technology. Florida power plants use water to cool their big turbine engines and pump the heated water back into the sea, creating a man-made hot spring. In winter the manatees gather around these power-plant outlets.

Manatee fat has another important use. Manatees are able to turn stored body fat into fresh water, as do other aquatic mammals such

A fat manatee is a healthy manatee.

as dolphins. It is known that manatees need fresh water. It is not known whether they need to obtain any of it by drinking, or if they can manufacture all they need through fat burn-off. They do drink fresh water when they have a chance. In water that is salty or brackish (a little bit salty), manatees seek out sources of fresh water. Florida manatees have been seen drinking from garden hoses running into a canal and from drainpipes. We saw many sea cows drinking from offshore springs.

Fat means safety for a manatee. The enormous size of the manatee is its only defense against predators. Manatees can't swim very fast. They have no sharp teeth, no claws, no poison. Fat, then, is the secret of their survival!

One-fifth of the species. The 240 manatees in this photo taken at the Florida Power and Light Company in Riviera show 20% of all living Florida manatees.

Drownproof

Mouth of the Crystal River, Florida
December 28
2 P.M.

Where the Crystal River meets the sea is a sandbar. There some limestone rocks stick up from the bottom and two waterlogged trees have become trapped. This is a manatee message center.

A bull in his seventh year, migrating from the sea to the warmth of the hot springs, enters the river and heads for the sandbar. The young bull has so many barnacles growing near his flipper that rangers guarding the Crystal River herd call him Barnacle.

Like the sea cows who came to the message center before him, he begins to rub against the rocks. With obvious delight Barnacle rubs the scent glands under his chin, beneath his flippers, and around his reproductive opening. By spreading his identifying scent around the message center, Barnacle is letting other manatees know he has come to Crystal River. He especially wants female manatees to know, because this year he is old enough to mate.

The young bull puts his bristly muzzle against a rock and moves his fleshy lips over it, taking a "smell-taste." He learns there are many females in the area but none of them are ready for breeding. Barnacle has swum

Scent marking in a manatee message center.

fifty miles today and he is tired, so he rests before moving upriver to the lovely warm water of the main boil.

It's about eight feet deep where the bull chooses to sleep. He rests in typical sleep posture, touching the bottom with his muzzle, flippers, and tail. About every ten minutes he rises to breathe. At the surface, the flaps on his nostrils open. He exhales, quickly inhales, closes the nose flaps, and sinks to the bottom.

Hours pass. Dusk creeps onto the river carrying the soft and gentle sounds of a Florida evening. Insects buzz, night herons call, and waves lap against the shores of countless small islands. Soon these sounds are joined by the hum of a distant motorboat. The hum grows louder, drowning out nature's evening chorus. The boat is coming in fast.

The napping manatee doesn't hear the boat. And in the twilight the pilot of the speeding boat doesn't see the manatee until it is too late.

Crash! A direct hit. The boat strikes the bull in the head, knocking him unconscious. Then deadly propellers rake across his back; whirring blades slice through the skin, taking huge chunks out of his back and severing part of his tail.

Motorboats can do terrible damage to a manatee's tail.

Blood is everywhere. Barnacle floats without moving. Then his broken body sinks into the water colored red with the blood from his horrible wounds. The cuts are many and deep, but in a few seconds the bleeding has stopped. In less than one minute the wounds have begun to close.

This superfast healing is due to a chemical in the blood of marine mammals that makes it clot when water hits it. (Human blood will not clot in water.) Quick-clotting blood is a marine adaptation that prevents manatees from bleeding to death underwater and keeps away predators that might be attracted to the smell of blood.

Barnacle's torn body lies motionless for five minutes. Then ten. Fifteen minutes—and no sign of movement. Twenty minutes have passed without Barnacle breathing. Will he drown?

Manatees can't drown. Breathing is not automatic to manatees as it is to land mammals. Manatees must remember to breathe. This safety mechanism protects them from accidentally letting water into their lungs, even when sleeping or unconscious. They are drownproof!

Although he cannot drown, Barnacle can suffocate. Marine mammals are able to go without breathing for a long time because their bodies are storehouses of oxygen. Their blood, like human blood, contains an oxygen-carrying protein called hemoglobin. In addition, marine mammals have large amounts of myoglobin, a protein that serves the same function in the muscles.

A manatee's body can also conserve oxygen by slowing down or even stopping body activities not essential to survival. Its digestive system and kidney functions can shut off, allowing more blood to flow to the brain and the heart, which then beats at a slower rate than normal.

Barnacle is beginning to move slowly. He is alive but in pain. With feeble strokes of his flippers he moves toward the air. His nose breaks the surface of the water and he breathes. Then he swims slowly toward the main spring.

The boat has not hit any vital organs. Barnacle's rocklike bones helped protect him, and none of them are broken. The long lungs, so close to the top of his back, were not injured. All Barnacle needs now is a safe place and recovery time. Crystal River Wildlife Refuge is the sanctuary he needs. In a few weeks his wounds will be healed.

"A" is for Ariel. Scientists have developed a painless method of branding captive manatees like Ariel.
It is called freeze burning.

The gentle, defenseless manatee has no worse enemy than us . . . and no better friend.

Man and Manatee

Crystal River Wildlife Refuge is a real place. Almost sold for a housing development in 1982, it was purchased by the Nature Conservancy. In 1983, the nine wild islands and the mighty springs became the first national wildlife refuge for manatees. They share it with a multitude of fish, turtles, dolphins, birds, otters, and humans.

Florida manatees have Crystal River and twenty other refuges. There are strong laws to protect them, and rangers to enforce the laws. But their numbers are declining.

Saving the manatee is an American challenge—one that we should be able to meet.

Manatees are adaptable. They can live in fresh or salt water. They can eat a variety of plants. They do not require big wilderness areas. Where they are not hunted they have no fear of humans and can coexist even in heavily populated areas.

But it is beyond their power to adapt to speeding boats and crushing barges, which account for one third of all deaths. Only humans can prevent boat collisions or accidents in flood-control gates.

Not as dramatic, but perhaps the biggest threat of all, is the increasing destruction of the sea-grass beds the manatees need for food. Laws prohibiting dumping, dredging, or filling of these underwater pastures are urgently needed.

With our help the manatee can survive. By saving an endangered species in our own country, we can help the world to see how important—and effective—animal protection can be.

This is the place to begin. No one is too young to get involved in causes that count. It is never too early to work for something that really matters.

Where to See Manatees

IN THE WILD

BLUE SPRING STATE PARK, Orange City.

CRYSTAL RIVER WILDLIFE REFUGE, Crystal River.

FLORIDA POWER AND LIGHT PLANT, Fort Lauderdale.

HOMOSASSA SPRING, Homosassa. Below the Nature World attraction.

TAMPA ELECTRIC COMPANY BIG BEND WALK, Tampa.

IN CAPTIVITY

Hurt or rescued manatees are sometimes raised in commercial oceanariums and can be viewed while being rehabilitated. The Marine Mammal Protection Act and the Endangered Species Act require that they be returned to the wild as soon as possible. These animals are the property of the American people and are under federal supervision.

EPCOT LIVING SEAS ATTRACTION, DISNEY WORLD, Orlando.

MIAMI SEAQUARIUM, Miami.

NATURE WORLD ATTRACTION, Homosassa.

SEA WORLD OF ORLANDO, Orlando.

Manatee Facts

Common Name: Florida Manatee (*man*-uh-tee) Male: bull. Female: cow. Baby: calf. Group: herd.

Scientific Name: Trichechus manatus latirostris

Size: Males and females same size. Average length: 10 feet. Average weight: 1,200 pounds. Record size: 13 ½ foot pregnant cow weighing 3,750 pounds (including twin calves).

Speed: Cruising 2 mph. Maximum 15 mph.

Color: Gray or gray-brown.

Behavior: Gentle. Slow moving. Solitary, although found in herds at hot water sources in winter. Shy and secretive. Nomadic.

Food: Sea grasses and freshwater plants. Eats 10 to 15% of body weight per day.

Habitat/Range: Shallow rivers, canals, and coastal areas of Florida. Clear or muddy water.

Life Span: Fifty years or longer.

Gestation: Thirteen months. One calf (occasionally twins) every three to five years.

Population: About 1,200.

Predators: Humans. Possibly sharks, alligators, and crocodiles, although undocumented.

Index